Ants

Published in the United States by
Gloucester Press, in 1981

Originated by David Cook and
Associates and produced by
The Archon Press Ltd
8 Butter Market
Ipswich

First Published in
Great Britain 1981 by
Hamish Hamilton Children's Books Ltd
Garden House, 57-59 Long Acre
London WC2E 9JZ

Printed in Great Britain by
W S Cowell Ltd
Butter Market, Ipswich

Certain illustrations originally published in
The Closer Look Series

Library of Congress
Catalog Card Number: 80-85049
ISBN: 0-531-03452-6

Ants

Consultant editor
Henry Pluckrose

Illustrated by
Tony Swift and David Cook

small world

Gloucester Press · New York · Toronto · 1981
Copyright © The Archon Press Ltd 1981

Although they look very different, ants and people have a lot in common. Ants live together in colonies where they all have different jobs to do. There are builder ants, farmer ants, gardener ants and hunter ants. There are even nurse ants for the young who are looked after for up to nine months. Despite there being so many different kinds of ants, they all look rather the same.

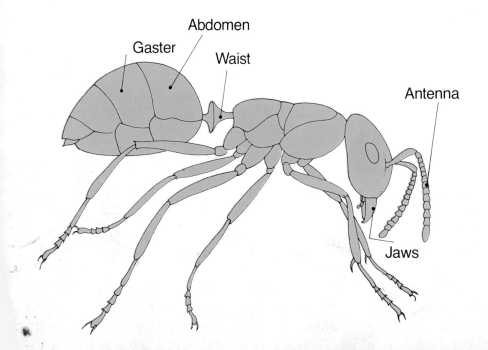

Gaster

Abdomen

Waist

Antenna

Jaws

In most colonies there are three
main types of ant to do these jobs.
The males are used only to mate
with (fertilize) the queen and then
they die.
The queen is the largest ant
and is the mother of the whole colony.
The workers do all the jobs that
keep the colony running smoothly.
The ants in this picture are workers.
Some are gathering food and some
are guarding the entrance to
their nest.

8

Once a year there is a lot of activity
around the nest.
In the evening two types of winged
ant will pour out of the nest
and fly away.
These are males and unmated queens.
They mate in the sky and then
drop to earth.

Once they have mated with the queens, the males soon die.
The mated queens shed their wings.
Then they dig a tunnel and start laying the eggs that will eventually become a new colony.

A queen breaking off her wings.

A queen tunneling underground and starting to lay her eggs.

The queen licks and takes care of
her eggs, laying more all the time.
The eggs hatch into grubs which
she feeds with her saliva.
They spin cocoons around themselves.
When this happens they are
called pupae.
When the pupae are ready to hatch
the queen tears the cocoons open
and the first small worker ants
appear.

Once enough workers have hatched, the
queen becomes the most pampered
member of the colony. The workers
feed and groom her so she can lay
many more eggs in comfort.
Now special nursery workers take
care of the young. They lick the eggs
and grubs, keeping them clean, well-fed
and at the right temperature
(not too hot and not
too cold).

Now the most important job for the
workers to do is to find food.
Ants eat plants and other insects and
a large colony needs a lot of food.
When ants find a caterpillar or wasp,
they bite it and spray the wound
with acid to paralyze it.
Then the ants cut it up and carry
it back to their nest for the grubs
and other members of the colony
to feed from.

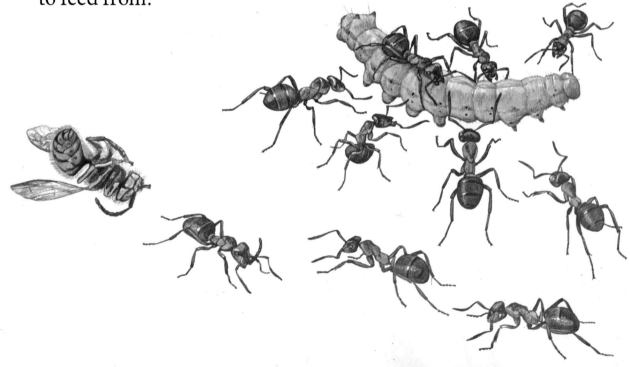

A group of small ants will sometimes
attack a single large ant by biting
its antennae and legs.

Yellow ants
attacking
a Wood ant.

Ants pass food on to one another by
"kissing". They have two stomachs,
one where food is stored for other
ants and one for their
own use.

During the "kiss" ants also pass on
the messages which tell them
what job to do.
These messages come from the
queen and the workers receive
them by licking her.

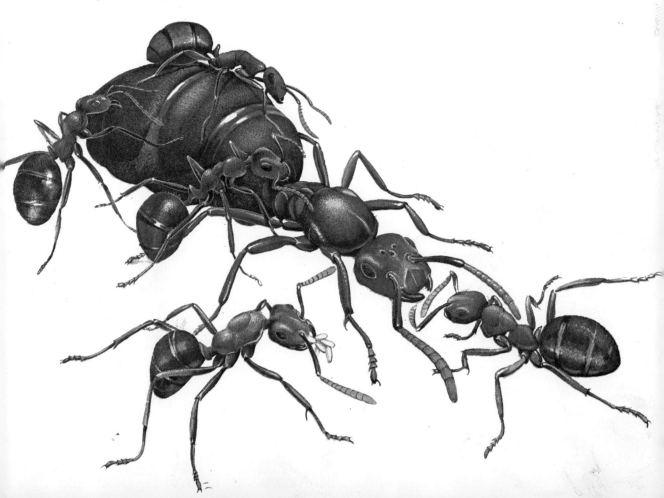

There can be as many as one million ants in a nest.

If you could look inside a nest, you would be able to see lots of things.

1. The queen laying eggs and nursery workers carrying them away.

2. A nursery for the grubs.

3. Nurses looking after the pupae.

4. New workers hatching from pupae.

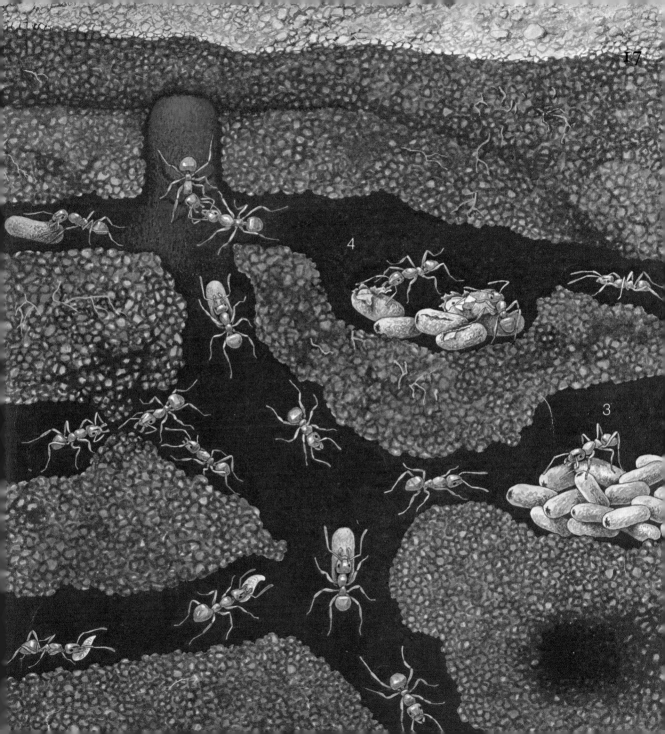

Ants do not always live in nests
underground.
Doorkeeper ants live inside plant stems.
Mudball ants build their nests in
trees and disguise them with plants.

Doorkeeper
ants.

Mudball ants
building their
nest.

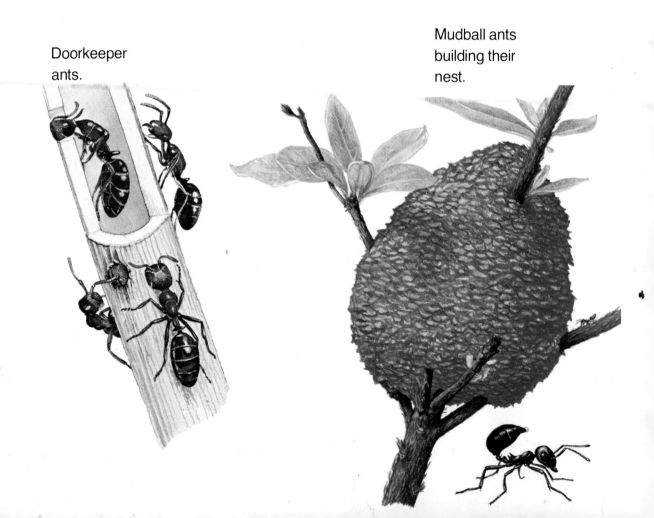

Tailor ants work together to build a
nest out of leaves. They use silk
which is produced by their grubs to
stitch the nest together.

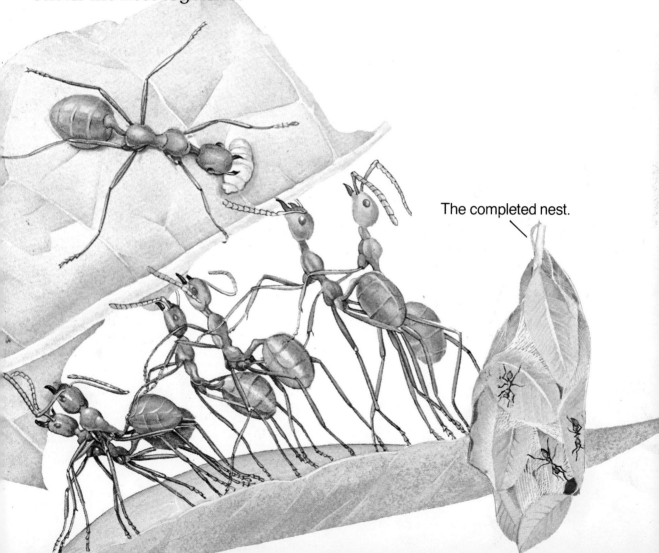

The completed nest.

Some ants are gardeners.
These Parasol ants cut down leaves
and take them down into underground
gardens.

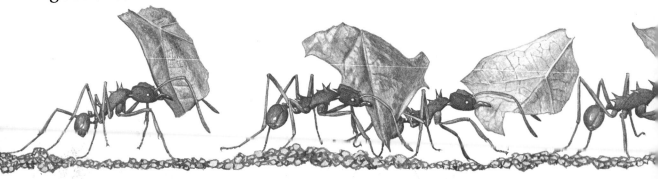

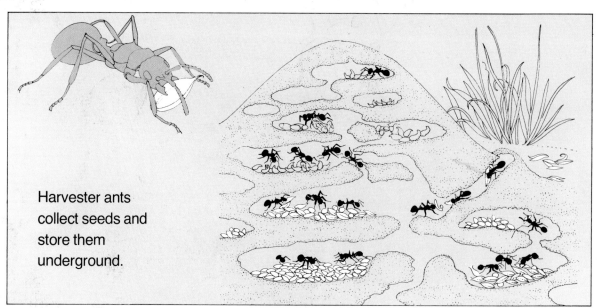

Harvester ants
collect seeds and
store them
underground.

Here the leaves are chewed up.
Then a fungus grows on the chewed
leaves and the Parasol ants feed
on the fungus.

Tiny insects called aphids produce a sweet substance called honeydew. Some ants from Australia and North America store this. When honeydew is plentiful, workers feed until their gasters become bloated and they can hardly move. Then they hang upside down and other ants use them as a honeypot when food is scarce.

The Blue butterfly lays its eggs on Wild Thyme. The eggs hatch into caterpillars which feed on the plant. If a caterpillar starts to wander, it will be found by ants. They like the taste of the sweet liquid it produces, and will take the caterpillar into their nest. Here the ants care for it and feed from it until the caterpillar hatches into a butterfly and flies away.

These are Army ants from Africa.
They are fierce hunters and travel
in great numbers looking for food.
They eat anything that cannot get
out of their path in time.
Some have even been known to
eat a horse which is tied to a post!

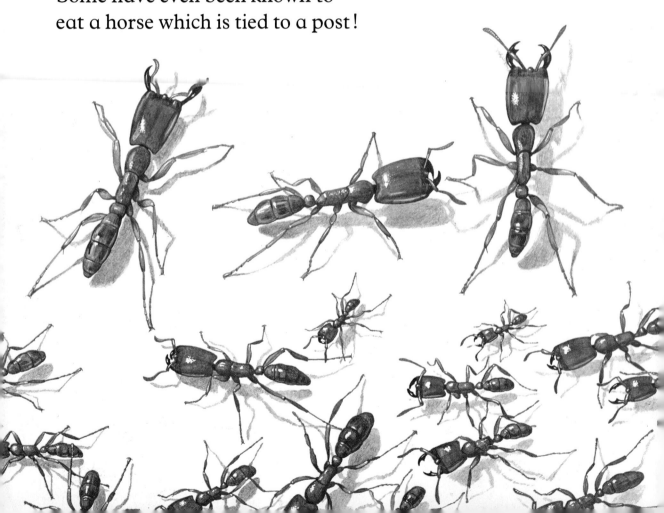

Army ants move in a dense column
with large soldier ants at the front
and sides for protection.
The column only stops marching for
the queen to lay her eggs.
As soon as the pupae hatch, they
move off again.

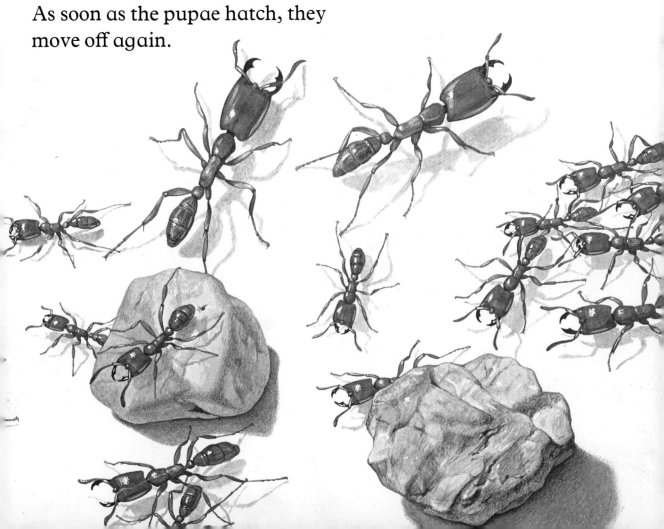

Red Amazon ants rely on black
worker slave ants to look after
them and their young in the nest.

1. The red Amazon
   ant attacks the black
   ant's nest and kills
   a worker.
2. It carries off a
   black pupa to
   its own nest.
3. When the black
   pupa hatch they
   look after the red
   Amazon ants.

A Blood-red ant queen, when ready
to lay her eggs, invades the nest
of certain black ants.
She steals some black pupae and
when they hatch, they think she is
their mother and look after her
red eggs.

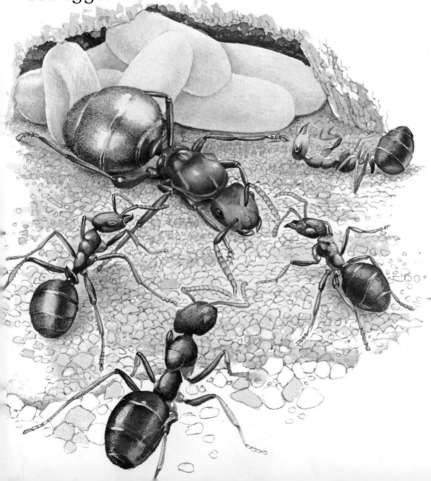

Ants are among the most interesting
of insects and live in a way that
seems very like our own.
Here are some of the more common
types of ant which can be found
all over the world.

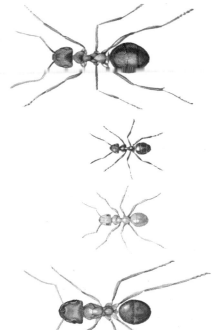

Wood ant from
North West Europe
and parts of Asia.

Black ant from
North America, Europe,
Middle East, Asia and
Japan.

Yellow ant from
Europe, North America
and Asia.

Blood-red ant from
Europe and parts of
Asia.

Amazon ant from
Southern Europe.

Index